HOW TO PLAY

WINNING

TENNIS

MARY HAWTON

Bookthrift Publications
New York

ACKNOWLEDGEMENTS

The publisher sincerely thanks Sportsman's
Corner, Dee Why, NSW, for their assistance in
supplying tennis equipment for photography.

This edition
Published by Bookthrift
One West 39th Street
New York, New York 10018

First published by
Paul Hamlyn Pty Limited
176 South Creek Road, Dee Why West
Australia 2099
First published 1979
© Copyright Paul Hamlyn Pty Limited 1979
Typeset by G.T. Setters Pty Limited
Printed in Hong Kong

ISBN: 78-61398
Library of Congress Catalog Card Number:
0-89673-005-0

CONTENTS

FOREWORD

This book will be of great benefit and learning value to tennis players of all ages. Tennis is a game for a lifetime. Young players certainly have greater scope for improvement, but there is always room for learning in everyone's tennis game, and I think this book is a great addition to all tennis library collections.

Mary is a tennis enthusiast, tennis administrator, experienced international player and national champion, and always a great exponent of the game, its style, technique and strategies.

Mary's experience in these areas over many years certainly makes her as a person of enthusiasm, one well qualified to write a good instructional book, such as this. I am sure it will help everyone who is interested in better tennis.

Ken Rosewall

INTRODUCTION

Anyone who has watched the high-powered battles of top-class players in championship matches will agree that tennis is a game of skill, speed and excitement. These ingredients can also be gained at a club level of tennis for the average player. Tennis is an international game played throughout the world. The reason why it is so popular is that it can be played by both sexes, and is regarded as a family game, a game of a lifetime: you can play from age eight to eighty. It is mentally stimulating as strategy plays such a big part in the game, and it can be enjoyable even if you are not a natural athlete.

Although this is a serious instructional book, it is written in the belief that most tennis enthusiasts play for pleasure, good health and relaxation. This is conveyed in the advice that greater expertise will give you the opportunity to participate in a wonderful sport played by millions, and introduce you to many new friends.

ABOUT THE GAME

ABOUT THE GAME

Tennis is a game played with rackets and balls in which individual players (for singles) or pairs (for doubles) compete against each other. It is played on a rectangular court divided across the center by a net. The surface of the court may be lawn, clay or any one of a number of synthetic materials.

Opposing players hit the ball backwards and forwards across the net. The aim is to hit the ball, in court, in a way that makes it impossible for the opposing player to return it. When a player commits a fault, or is unable to return a ball, points are awarded to the other side.

THE COURT

The Playing Area: The court for both singles and doubles is a rectangle divided into two equal halves by a net. A singles court measures 78 ft (23.77 m) long and 27 ft (8.23 m) wide. A doubles court is the same length but 36 ft (10.97 m) wide.
The Net: The net is suspended across the center of the court. It is 3 ft (91 cm) high at the center and 3 ft 6 in (107 cm) high at the posts. A handle attached to one of the posts enables the height of the net to be adjusted.
The Sidelines: The lines bounding the sides of the court for either singles or doubles play.
The Baselines: The lines bounding the ends of the court.

The Center Line: The line dividing the court width into two equal halves to form the service courts.
The Service Courts: The areas into which the server must *serve* the ball at the beginning of each point in order to put the ball into play.
The Service Lines: The lines parallel to the net and 21 ft (6.4 m) from it.
Service Sidelines: The lines forming the boundary of the service courts at the right and left hand sides.
Alley or Tramlines: The area between the singles and doubles sidelines.
The Center Marks: The short extensions of the center lines bisecting each of the baselines.
The Lines on the Court:
Center Service Line 2 in (5 cm) wide.
Center Mark on Baseline 4 in (10 cm) long and 2 in (5 cm) wide.
All other lines should be not less than 1 in (2.5 cm) and not more than 2 in (5 cm) wide, except the baseline which may be 4 in (10 cm) in width. All measurements are made to the outside of the lines.

THE RACKET

The racket must consist of a frame of any material, weight, size or shape and strings which are either alternately interlaced or bonded where they cross; strings must be

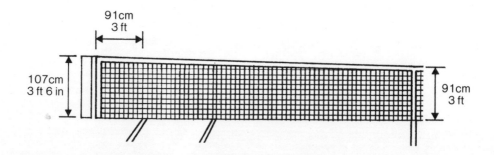

91cm
3 ft

107cm
3 ft 6 in

91cm
3 ft

connected to the frame. If there are attachments, they must be for wear and tear purposes only and should not alter the flight of the ball.

This rule has recently been introduced on an experimental basis; it will be reconsidered at the 1979 Annual General Meeting of the International Tennis Federation.

THE BALL

The ball must be stitchless and made to the following specifications:

Diameter: maximum 2⅝ in (6.667 cm), minimum 2½ in (6.35 cm).

Weight: maximum 2¹/₁₆ oz (58.5 grams), minimum 2 oz (56.7 grams).

Bounce: when dropped from a height of 100 in (254 cm) upon a concrete base — maximum 58 in (147 cm), minimum 53 in (135 cm).

GAME, SET AND MATCH

A tennis match is a contest consisting of an odd number of sets in which the winner is the player winning the most sets. The maximum number of sets in a men's match is five and in a women's match three. The first player or pair to reach a sum of six games wins the set. If the score levels at five each, then the first player or pair to be two games ahead is the winner. When the match is finished the winner's score is always quoted first. For example, player A won a five set match with the score 4-6, 6-4, 2-6, 6-3, 6-4. You know he has won the match by three sets to two.

Ball in and Out of Play

The ball is in play if it bounces inside the court area or if any part of it hits any part of the line. It is only out if there is a space between where it bounces and the line.

Rules of Play

There are 38 rules of tennis and many are lengthy. The main ones are given here. The players toss for service or choice of ends at the beginning of a match. The winner may elect to receive first, rather than serve, in which case he or she has the choice of ends as well. Players then take it in turn to serve and throughout the match the players must change ends after every odd game (after the first, third, fifth and so on). Play must be continuous and the umpire's decision is final.

The Ball Remains in Play When:

1. The player leans over the net to hit the ball after it has bounced on the player's side of the net and then rebounded to the opponent's side of the net. This is a good return provided the ball has not bounced twice before the player hits it and provided neither the player nor his racket or clothing touches the net.
2. The player hits the ball onto the top of the net and it bounces into the opponent's court. This also applies if it hits the net post.
3. The player hits the ball and it touches any part of the boundary line.
4. The player hits the ball around the net post and it lands within the boundaries of the court.
   (An inexpensive book *Rules of Tennis* is a very handy book to take to your match in case queries arise. This can be obtained from your local tennis association.)

The Ball is Out of Play When:

1. The player fails to return the ball over the net or hits it out of the court.
2. The ball bounces twice before returning over the net.
3. The player leans over the net to hit the ball before it crosses to the players side of the net.
4. The player strikes the ball more than once to return it.
5. The player hits the serve on the fly (full) before it bounces.
6. The player allows the racket to leave his hand to hit the ball.
7. The player touches the ball with his body or anything he wears or carries except his racket, even if he is outside the boundaries of the court.
8. The ball hits the ground, a permanent fixture, or any object outside the lines of opponent's court.
9. The player or his racket touches the net, net post, net band, center strap or the ground inside the opponent's court while the ball is in play.
10. The player touches the ball with his racket when it already has been hit by his partner. (Refer to Glossary for Footfault rules and definitions.)

HOW TO SCORE

Tennis is played for points, which you gain only when you make a winning shot or when your opponent loses a point. The first point gives you a score of 15, the second point takes you to 30, the third point takes you to 40. The fourth point you win takes you to "game" if your opponent's score is less than 40, or to "advantage" if your opponent has also scored 40.

Your opponent also scores for the points he wins, therefore, it is possible for your scores to be even: (15-15) — this is called fifteen all; (30-30) thirty all; (40-40) deuce (not forty all). Beyond deuce the method of scoring changes. The player (singles) or players (doubles) winning the next point after deuce go to "advantage", the call being advantage server or advantage receiver, or in the case of an international match advantage Australia or advantage U.S.A.

From "advantage" the score goes to "game", if the advantage player or pair wins the next point, or back to deuce if they lose it. The deuce advantage score has no limitations and is repeated until either side wins two consecutive points.

The first player to win six games (such as 6-4) wins the set, except when five games all has been reached, in which case one player must be two games ahead (such as 7-5 or 12-10).

A zero score is called "love", and the server's point is called first, so if the score is "fifteen love" you know the server has won the first point. If "love forty" is called you know the server has lost the first three points.

Tie breakers have been an added innovation to the scoring system in recent years; this was added to limit the length of matches because of tight scheduling for television. If a tennis match reaches six games all, a series of points are played breaking up the service routine, giving each side even service chances.

COURT COURTESIES

Tennis is an international game and the same rules apply everywhere. This is also true of the courtesies. If you observe them you will be welcomed as a player who makes the game enjoyable for your partner and for your opponents and you will receive many invitations to play.

When an opposing team comes to your club, treat them as you would guests in your home. It is your duty to welcome them, entertain them and say goodbye. Always be a good guest when you are visiting other clubs. If you play competition, remember you are representing your club, not just yourself.

Do not query the umpire's decision. The calls usually even out: if he makes an error your end, he will probably make one the other end too.

When the point is finished, return the balls straight to the server. Try not to lose your temper: refrain from such antics as throwing your racket, kicking or slamming the ball. If your opponent sees you are agitated, he knows he has you worried. This will give him added confidence.

At the conclusion of the match remember to thank the umpire, and always leave the court with your opponent.

Never walk behind a court when a rally is in progress.

TECHNIQUES AND SKILLS

THE GRIPS

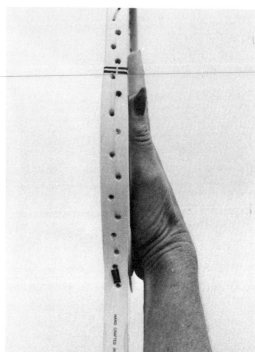

1 *Finding the grip.*

You will soon learn that if your grips are not correct your strokes will be limited and probably inaccurate. A good grip is designed to give you several advantages. Strength for power, flexibility and naturalness for touch. Incorrect grips usually limit one of these aspects.

There is very little time to change grips in a quick exchange from the baseline and it is almost impossible at the net. Therefore, it is advisable for the beginner to use an Eastern or "shake hands" grip for the forehand and an Eastern backhand grip which is a slight change for the backhand strokes.

THE EASTERN FOREHAND

To achieve the Eastern forehand grip, hold the racket in your left hand perpendicular to the ground. Place your right hand flat against the strings and slowly bring your hand down to the handle and grip it. In other words merely shaking hands with the racket (your fingers should wrap around the racket naturally and be slightly apart). Do not grip your racket too tightly. It is like holding a little bird: if you hold it too loosely it will fly out of your hand and if you hold it too tightly you will kill it. The same applies to a tennis stroke.

THE EASTERN BACKHAND

For your backhand grip you now have to get your wrist behind the racket. Holding it in your shake hands forehand grip, move your hand slightly to the left: the racket should now be diagonally in your hand and your fingers comfortably spread. The "V" between your thumb and forefinger will be slightly to the left of the racket handle. This backhand ground stroke and volley grip is also the serve and smash grip.

2 *Finding the grip.*

THE EASTERN FOREHAND GRIP

THE EASTERN BACKHAND GRIP

1 *Eastern forehand.*

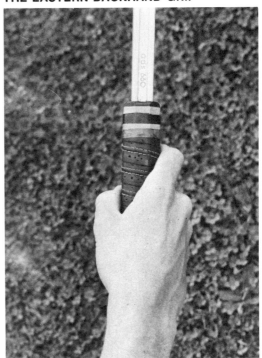

1 *Eastern backhand.*

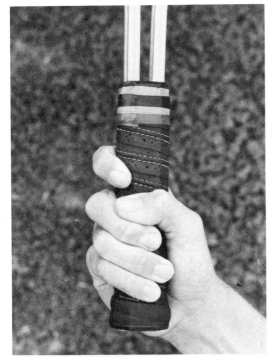

2 *Eastern forehand — finger position.*

2 *Eastern backhand — finger position.*

1 *Continental grip.*

THE CONTINENTAL GRIP

As your game improves you may wish to change very slightly to the all purpose grip called the Continental grip. This grip is in between the Eastern forehand and backhand grip. The heel of your hand will be almost on top of the racket with the "V" of your forefinger and thumb very slightly to the left of the top of the racket. The Continental grip requires a fairly strong arm since the wrist is not directly behind the racket as it is with the Eastern grips. If you want to be a top line volleyer then you should use **one** grip for your net game, either the Continental or the Eastern backhand. Sedgeman, Gonzales, Rosewall and Hoad are just some of the tennis stars who use these grips.

If you have started with the wrong grip do not try to change it dramatically, or the correct grip will feel awkward to you. When you practice just slightly change it until that position becomes comfortable and then change a little further.

2 *Continental grip — finger position.*

READY POSITION

1 *Waiting position, with weight on balls of feet, racket out in front.*

This corresponds to the starter on the running blocks. Any worthy opponent will hit the ball away from you. A quick step off the mark is vital and is impossible from an upright position. To check this make sure your shoulders are hanging over your toes, knees should be bent, and the weight on the balls of your feet with your eyes on the flight of the ball. The racket should be held waist high and straight out in front with the head a little above the wrist. This will ensure you do not favour either forehand or backhand. You should now be crouched like a panther ready to leap at the prey which in this case is the ball. The name of the game in tennis is to judge where the ball is going to bounce and be there in a stationary position with the racket back ready as the ball bounces. To do this, you must watch the ball leave your opponent's racket. This will allow you to start moving immediately to the exact spot where the ball will land. When the ball bounces there is a split second when it reaches the top of the bounce. This is the moment you should try to hit the ball. When you have completely finished the stroke return quickly to the center of the court just behind the baseline, taking up the ready position for the next shot. When your game advances you will be able to improve your anticipation, by judging the type of shot your opponent is allowed to hit from the position you have forced him into.

THE STROKES

THE FOREHAND

FOREHAND

Almost all beginners commence playing tennis by learning to hit a forehand drive. There are three types of forehand strokes: the flat, the slice and the topspin drives. The flat drive is the first one to learn as the basics for the others are the same.

Check your grip (page 14) and get into the ready position (page 17).

PREPARATION

Early preparation is the most important part of a forehand drive. If you prepare late the entire stroke will be out of co-ordination. It will then develop into a defensive shot, as you will be forced to hit the ball on the down instead of the top of the bounce. Immediately you see the ball coming to the forehand side you should turn your shoulders and pivot your hips, so that your left shoulder is pointing in the direction of the flight of the ball. Your weight will be on your right foot. So, as the ball leaves your opponent's racket you will be in the ready position with your racket at waist level. Keep your head looking over your left shoulder with your eyes on the ball. As you move towards the ball, take your racket back to arm's length, and at waist level. At full stretch your racket should be no more than at right angles to the net. You should plan to contact the ball just in front of your front foot.

STEP TOWARDS THE NET

When you reach the ball, step towards the net, in a sideways position, making sure your front foot is firmly planted. Your left leg will give you the solid base to hit off, and this is the only position in which you can achieve the proper weight transfer. Swing your racket forward to hit the ball at waist height and at the peak of the bounce, as though you were sweeping a row of cups off a long table. If the ball is low bend your knees until your eyes are on the same level as the ball, and this will automatically bring the plane of the racket swing down to the flight of the ball.

1 *Preparation — turn shoulders and pivot.*

2 *Backswing — step towards the net.*

HIT AND FOLLOW THROUGH

As you start to swing forward, keep your head down and your eyes on the ball up to and beyond the moment of contact. Hit and follow through from low to high, finishing with the racket head facing the spot you wish the ball to go. Your racket head should finish at least as high as eye level. The low to high hitting action and follow through will give you a slight natural top spin to the ball to get it over the net and yet keep it in the court. When you are practicing try placing the ball in different positions. The basics are the same for each shot, however if you wish to hit the ball across-court take the ball a little earlier and slightly further out in front. The drill for the forehand is: ready position, preparation, step, hit and follow through. This can be done at home without the ball until it becomes a reflex action.

Vitas Gerulaitis plays a great forehand with excellent fundamentals. He uses an Eastern forehand grip. His first movements of both shoulders and feet to the side are exceptionally fast. His backswing is short and neat and he uses his full shoulder power, and plays the shot completely side on to the net, which gives him good disguise. Because of his speed to the ball he is always well positioned early and consequently can take the ball early. He uses his legs and body weight to full advantage and has a very good follow through.

MOST COMMON FOREHAND ERRORS

1. Preparing late: You must watch the ball from your opponent's racket and start preparing as you run to the spot where the ball will land. It is too late to start swinging once the ball has bounced.

2. Moving too slowly to the ball: You must start moving to the ball the moment the ball leaves your opponent's racket. The first quick turn of your shoulder in the direction of the ball will help your take off. If you arrive late you will not be able to hit the ball on the rise or the top of the bounce.

3 *Hit with arm straight.*

4 *Follow through from low to high.*

3. Not stepping towards the net: If you do not step with your front foot forward and sideways to the net you will not be able to transfer your body weight into the ball. Make this your solid base to hit off and it will help keep your knees bent.

4. Cutting off the follow through: If you do not hit through the ball you will lose your depth and accuracy. A complete follow through will automatically keep you watching the ball longer and not looking up to see where your opponent is, which is fatal.

FOREHAND CHECKLIST
1. Wait low with your head forward for quick take off.
2. Take your racket back as soon as possible, ready to come forward when you reach the ball.
3. Bend your knees for a low ball.
4. Slip out in front and bring your body sideways to the net and hit through the ball.

THE BACKHAND

1 *Waiting position with knees bent.*

2 *Shoulder turn and pivot.*

The backhand is neglected by far too many beginners because they find it difficult to master. This neglect is very costly as a weak backhand leaves a player very vulnerable and his opponent will exploit it to the fullest. The backhand is a more natural stroke and can be easier to learn than a forehand if the correct fundamentals are used. When you hit a forehand the left shoulder can pull away and cramp the follow through, but the backhand is made with a swing away from the body. The correct grip for the backhand is essential. You must get your wrist behind the racket, or the stroke will be a push with no power (see GRIP, page 14).

The first movement for a backhand is vital. As the ball leaves your opponent's racket, you should start your shoulder turn and pivot the hips, using your left hand to take the racket across. Your eyes must look up the court over your right shoulder as you start to move in the direction of the ball. You should move sideways and forward into the ball, not backwards, arriving at the spot at which the ball is about to bounce. The swing should be straight back, with the arm tucked against your right hip. It is impossible to hit a good backhand with a bent elbow. Your right shoulder has to be at full stretch as if you were reaching for something

behind your back. This movement can be practiced in front of a mirror until it becomes a reflex action. To check the position see if your right shoulder is behind your right foot. You should plan to hit the ball just in front of your forward hip. If you are properly prepared, you should be able to hit the ball on the top of the bounce about waist level and so gain maximum power and accuracy. If the ball is lower than waist level you should use your knees as an elevator until your racket is at the level of the ball. Do not bend from the waist or drop the head of the racket. Step towards the net, making sure your front foot is firmly planted before the hit, as your legs become the solid base to hit off. This is where you gain your body power. As you start to swing forward, make sure you keep your head down and your eyes on the ball. Follow through from low to high, finishing with the racket head pointing to the spot you wish the ball to go. The shoulder should bring the racket into the ball. If you hit the ball up in the air it means the racket has gone ahead of your shoulder and you have pushed with the arm, instead of swinging. The finish of the stroke is the check point. If the racket is pointing to the side fence instead of the back fence, you have either not had your shoulder at full stretch on the backswing or

3 *Backswing, taking racket straight back.*

4 *Shift weight forward, hitting ball out in front.*

you have taken your eyes off the ball. If you prepare late the entire stroke will be out of co-ordination, and if the ball goes in the court at all it will be a defensive shot, as you will have had to hit the ball on the down and not the top of the bounce.

Ken Rosewall hits a classic backhand stroke because his fundamentals are perfect. His movement to the backhand side commences like lightning. The preparation is fast with a low front shoulder, drawn back with arm fully extended. His speed to the ball is extraordinary and this enables him to hit the ball very early (on the rise or top of the bounce). Both his legs are solidly placed, with the knees always bent to the low ball. His shoulder throws his racket at the ball like a catapult (sling shot) firing, leaving the head in a still position and so allowing his eyes to have clear vision for perfect timing.

MOST COMMON BACKHAND ERRORS

1. Not watching the ball: It is vital in a backhand to watch the ball from the time it leaves your opponent's racket to the moment of impact. You may get away with hitting a

5 *Follow through from low to high.*

forehand in an open stance, that is facing the net, but you will not with a backhand. Keep your eyes on the flight of the ball as you run towards it, looking over your front shoulder, watching the ball until you have finished the shot.

2. Not turning shoulder and pivoting: When you decide to take the ball on your backhand you must start turning your shoulder immediately and pivot from the waist. This throws the weight on to your backhand side, giving you a quick take off.

3. Not bending your knees: Your racket must come forward at the same level as the ball, that is why it is easier to take it at waist level. If you have arrived late to the ball or the bounce is low you must bend down with your knees and not from the waist. This will also bring your eyes down close to the ball. You will need the power of your body weight coming forward and you will only attain this if you have a solid base on the ground.

4. Pushing the ball: Many players have a tendency to push the backhand just to get it over. By the time you are coming into the shot your shoulder should be fully stretched and your arm straight. Your back should be almost facing your opponent. Throw your shoulder at and through the ball but do not try to stretch.

BACKHAND CHECKLIST

1. Turn your shoulders and pivot your hips with your racket and arm at full stretch and close to the body.
2. Move quickly to where the ball is about to bounce.
3. Step with your right foot just before you hit the ball.
4. Throw your racket at the ball, leading with your shoulder.
5. Follow through and finish with the racket pointing at the spot you want the ball to go.

THE SERVE

1 *Stance — weight even and racket resting on left hand.*

There are three varieties of serves: the flat, the slice and the American twist or top spin. The flat serve is the first one to learn. Once this is mastered the others may be added to your repertoire. The grip for your serve is either the Eastern backhand grip or the Continental grip (pages 15-16).

Once you have the right grip you should work on your stance. Generally the feet should be wide enough apart to have the weight of the body evenly distributed on both feet. You must stand behind the base line, but the distance depends on the height of the individual. The main thing is to be relaxed and comfortable with a solid base. You should stand with your feet at about a 70° angle to the net; in other words do not stand at right angles or square on to the net. Your feet should form a line in the direction you wish the ball to go.

When you commence your serve, rest the throat of your racket on your left hand. Both hands should start moving together and be at the same height as you go through the various stages of the swing to the moment of impact.

2 *Start of swing and ball toss.*

3 *Arms at same level during swing.*

The most important and difficult part of the serve is the placing of the ball in the air, because it is done by the left hand and most people do not have the same control they do with the right hand. All great servers have a perfect ball throw. The throw up or toss should be slightly to the right and forward.

THE TOSS

For those with a crooked toss perhaps you could think of lifting the ball up or just placing it up. If you let the ball fall to the ground it should be about six inches (15 cm) to the right and about a foot (30 cm) ahead of your front toe. You can practice this at home until you are able to place the ball in the air and have it fall in the same spot every time. As a serve is a throwing action the easiest way to learn the swing is to have a number of balls, pick them up one at a time and throw them overarm into the court. Then, pick up the racket the same way as the ball and "throw" the ball off the racket as an extension of your hand.

Another way to get the feel of the swing is to take an old racket, stand on the service line and try to throw it up and over the net as far as you can. Then practice the swing without the ball and watch where the racket head comes at the top of the swing. This should be slightly to the right and forward of your body. When your body is fully extended, the point at which you have stopped at the top of the swing is the point of contact. If you make a natural throwing action you will automatically come up to contact the ball with your arm straight and your racket head flat.

The position of the body at this stage should present nearly a straight line from the bottom of your right heel to the top of your racket. Now try swinging and lifting the ball into the correct position, co-ordinating with the racket head. If you extend both arms up together you will notice the distance you have to lift the ball. It is essential to have your left arm straight to give the throwing arm time to complete the swing. The hit must be up and out, never down. Keep your head up and both eyes to a point on the

4 *Left arm fully extended.*

5 *Racket in ready throwing position.*

ball at the moment of impact and at least six inches (15 cm) through the hit. The shoulder as in all tennis strokes should lead the swing and after throwing your racket up and out at the ball your shoulder should pull you into the court.

The swing will naturally finish on the left side of the body. In your ready to serve position you should look down the court and decide precisely where you wish the ball to go. Take a mental picture of this and do not look down the court again. Remember the court never moves, but both the ball and your racket are moving and therefore require your entire concentration for split second timing.

Many champions have perfected their serves by practicing in front of a mirror. I think most tennis players will agree the best service in the world has been that of Pancho Gonzales. It is interesting to note that all the fundamentals of his serve are correct. Backhand grip which gives maximum wrist action, weight evenly balanced at the commencement, a completely relaxed throwing arm, perfect ball toss with left

arm fully extended, and head lifted back to allow the throwing shoulder to come through and both eyes to a point on the ball for the hit.

MOST COMMON SERVE ERRORS

1. The erratic service toss: It is important to consistently place the ball in the air in the same place. This must be practiced along with the swing. The best cure for this is to practice without the racket, marking a circle in front and slightly to the right of your left (front) foot, and checking to see if the ball lands in this circle. If you find this difficult, check to see if your fingers are relaxed and not holding the ball too tightly. You may also be releasing the ball too early or flicking it up with your wrist. Make sure your front arm is fully stretched.

2. Trying for too much power: Do not try for too much speed before you have accuracy. By trying for extra power you will increase the chances of overhitting the ball or netting it; better to get it in than serve a fault.

6 *The hit — body fully stretched at contact point.*

7 *Shoulder pressing through after the hit.*

3. Not leaning into the ball: Make sure the ball is far enough in front of you to lean into it. If you watch the champions such as Roscoe Tanner and John Newcombe, you will see how much body power they are getting into the shot by leaning into the court as they hit a powerful serve.

4. Rushing the serve: Take your time on the serve. Do not let your opponent hassle you into serving before you are ready. Take your aim and do not look down the court again, after all it will not move. Pay strict attention to the ball to enable split-second timing. Hit up and out, not down.

3. Place the ball up with a straight arm, at the height of your racket at full stretch.
4. Hit up and out at the ball with your head up until after the hit.

SERVE CHECKLIST

1. Take your time. Your opponent cannot hit the ball until you allow him to. Any errors are of your own making.
2. Hold the ball lightly in your fingers and keep your racket arm relaxed.

THE SMASH

1 *Sideways to the net with head up and eyes on the ball.*

2 *Point hand at ball, racket in throwing position.*

The grip for the overhead smash is the same as for the serve; that is either the Eastern backhand or Continental grip (see GRIPS, page 14). It is a more difficult stroke than the serve as you have to move quickly into position while the ball is still in the air. The judgement of where the ball will land is the most difficult part. For the beginner it is best to have someone lob to you and just catch the ball with your upstretched hand. You should catch it a little to the right and just in front of your left foot with the arm fully extended. Do this until you have a perfectly timed catch and then go back to your racket. If you cannot catch it you will not be able to hit it. The swing is similar to a serve; in fact the only difference in the action is that there is no need to swing your racket arm down and back as you place the ball in the air, so the swing is shorter. The action is as though you were throwing the racket over the back fence. As soon as you see the ball leaving your opponent's racket in an elevated position you should run back from the net, at the same time keeping your eye on the ball and get behind the flight of the ball. Turn sideways to the net before you begin the stroke. To help set your shoulders and head for a good throwing action, point your left hand up at the ball. You should set yourself in a position under the ball so that if it continued to drop it would hit you on the chin (or between the eyes). When the ball is a few feet above your head swing the racket forward and contact the ball in the center of the racket with your body fully stretched. The hit should be up and out as for the serve, with the racket finishing on the left side of the body. Try to hit the ball on the fly (full) unless it is past the service line, where it is better to let it bounce.

If a lob goes over your head and you cannot smash, you should play a lob back, unless you have time to set yourself to play a normal ground stroke or a bouncing smash. If you are missing your smash, it is because you are not ready early enough or you have taken your eyes off the ball. Always ask your opponent to send up a few lobs in the warm up of your match.

3 *Arm and racket at full stretch.*

4 *Follow through.*

MOST COMMON OVERHEAD SMASH ERRORS

1. Not positioning yourself under the ball: The judgement of moving to the ball and waiting under the flight, with the body placed sideways, needs a lot of practice. You should be in a stationary position, and if the ball continued to fall it would hit you on the chin.

2. Taking a long swing: A short comfortable swing is all you need. Just take your racket back in the throwing position, and concentrate on hitting the ball in the center of the strings.

3. Taking your eyes of the ball: It is easy to take your eye off the ball in a smash, particularly if you rush it in an attempt to hit it away from your opponent. Keep your head up and watch the ball hit the strings. Hit up and out, not down, and do not try to cramp the smash.

4. Lack of practice: The smash needs as much practice as any other shot and there are not many chances to smash in a match. This means you will have to have someone lob you hundreds of balls in your practice sessions.

OVERHEAD SMASH CHECKLIST

1. Move quickly under the ball so that it would hit you on the chin if it continued to fall.
2. Hit the ball in the air unless it is too high or deep or you have not positioned yourself under it.
3. Use a short backswing turning sideways to the net, pointing your free hand at the ball.
4. Hit up and out at the ball at the point of contact, with your arm and racket at full stretch.

THE LOB

1 *Sideways to the net — short backswing.*

2 *Racket ready to come under the ball.*

The lob, forehand and backhand, is the most underrated stroke in tennis. All champions have it in their repertoire. It should be practiced along with the other strokes.

The lob may be used in both attack and defense. The attacking lob is mostly used when your opponent is at the net and you want to force him back or catch him unaware. In singles it should be mainly hit to your opponent's backhand side. Hit it a little higher than jumping reach and as close to the baseline as possible. When playing doubles and returning from the forehand court, one of the best attacking shots in the game is the lob over the net player, deep into the server's backhand court. If the server is following his serve to the net, his partner has to run back and it gives you the opportunity to follow your lob to the net. This now puts you in the attacking position. Should the server elect not to follow his serve in, he has to turn his body and run to the backhand side which still puts him in a defensive position. The backhand court player should only use the lob as a surprise return to stop the server getting in too close to the net

and keep him guessing, because you are now lobbing to both their forehand and smash side. A defensive lob is used when you are forced into difficulties by your opponent's good shot. Anytime you are forced off the court it is best to lob deeply to give you a chance to return to the center of the court. A lob is also handy against a baseliner who is out-hitting you in rally exchanges. Send down a few lobs to the baseline, preferably to the corners, and this will quite likely break up his or her rhythm.

Ken Rosewall, Rod Laver and John Newcombe have won more matches with great lobs than any other players I have seen. Watch how a clever tactical lob gets a top class player out of trouble.

MOST COMMON LOB ERRORS

1. Lobbing short: If you lob short you are giving the point away as any worthy opponent will smash it for a winner. Aim your lob to land just inside the baseline. If you aim for just over your opponent's head and you are a little short or the wind brings it back you are in trouble.

THE VOLLEY

3 *Full follow through, finishing with racket high.*

2. Standing flat on: If you do not stand sideways to play the ball as in a normal ground stroke you will not be able to disguise the shot. Look at the ball and not the opposition, giving them the impression you are about to play a passing shot. If you lift your head to check the other player's position you will give away the element of surprise.

3. Cutting short the follow through: The longer you can keep the ball on your racket the deeper and more accurate your lob will be. You must hit up and under the ball with a full follow through, finishing as high as your shoulder will go.

LOB CHECKLIST

1. Aim for the baseline by hitting up and through the ball.
2. Hit it like a ground stroke to disguise the shot.
3. Watch the ball until you see it hit your racket strings.
4. Follow through with shoulder high.

The volley is considered a prime offensive shot for furthering your attack no matter what the level of your game. Even if you are an average club player and do not follow your serve to the net, you will still find it a great advantage when you can approach the net and end the point with a winning volley. While the volley is an easy stroke to make if correctly conducted, it is the most difficult if the fundamentals are wrong. The basic learning grip is the same as the forehand and backhand drives. However as there is less time to prepare for a net shot, most advanced players use the same grip for both forehand and backhand volleys. This is the Continental grip (see page 16). If it feels comfortable and you can manage it from the beginning it is advisable to do so. Before even attempting a volley the beginner should practice catching the ball. It must be caught in front of the body with a firm wrist and with the head at ball level. This practice gives the hand/eye co-ordination needed. The correct waiting position for the volley is more important than any other stroke and footwork is very important at the net. It is essential to be on your toes with the body weight forward, head and shoulders in a low position and the knees bent. Visualize a panther crouched ready to leap for the ball. The racket should be held out in front at chin level, and the elbows tucked in. As the volley is a "punch" it resembles the basics of a boxer in the ring, keeping up the hands which become your guard.

There is no real swing for a volley. The racket should not go back more than two feet (60 cm). The pivoting of your body will provide most of the backswing required. The shorter the swing the more control you have of your racket, and you get the power out of your volley from your opponent's shot. Many players are frightened of net play because the ball is coming at them with great speed. Remember the boxer: if you swing your racket behind you or drop your guard, you will be knocked out. Turn your shoulders and pivot, only now the racket and hand are up and ready to go forward and catch the ball on the racket strings. Step towards the

THE FOREHAND VOLLEY

1 *Waiting position, head and shoulders forward.*

2 *Turn shoulder and pivot with short backswing.*

net with your forward shoulder pointing towards the ball, hitting the ball at least six inches (15 cm) in front of your body. Follow through, keeping your eyes on the ball until the racket is fully extended. At the finish of the stroke your racket head should be facing the spot you wish the ball to go. Return immediately to your ready position.

Many average players are able to hit a good volley when the ball is above the top of the net. It is much more difficult to volley though when the ball is lower than the net, as you are forced to make a defensive shot by hitting up. If the ball is low you must bend your knees so your hitting position is the same for a waist high as for a low volley. That is, racket above the wrist and hand. Your eyes must be down on the level of the ball to give you perfect timing.

By the time you come to learn the volley you should be automatically watching the ball from your opponent's racket. Therefore, you should never be caught with the ball coming straight at you, because your decision for making either a forehand or backhand volley should have been made the second it left your opponent's racket.

The golden rule for a volley is that it must be played off your front foot. If you step back you have prepared too late.

When playing singles, the correct position for volleying is on the center line about halfway between the service line and the net. You are now in a ready position to move in if you get an easy shot and your opponent will not be able to lob over your head. After the first volley you should always move forward. Every foot you move forward from inside the service line increases the angles available for your next shot. Do not move, however, until the ball is leaving your opponent's racket, otherwise he will change his hitting direction.

In doubles you should stand almost in the middle of the service court on the side your partner is serving to.

MOST COMMON VOLLEY ERRORS

1. Wrong waiting position: The crouched waiting position is essential. There is less time for taking off than with any other shot. You will have to leap to the sidelines and up for a

3 *Step forward and hit.*

4 *Follow through, racket facing the spot you wish the ball to go.*

smash. You cannot get the same distance if you stand in an upright position. Your head needs to be forward and your eyes on the level of the ball which is usually about your opponent's waist height.

2. Long backswing: You do not have time to take a long backswing for a volley, and doing so will cut down on your accuracy, as most of the time you will be hitting with the ball behind your line of vision. There is enough pace on your opponent's shot to allow your punch volley, meeting the ball out in front of your body, to give you good depth and power.

3. Poor anticipation: Since there is little time to make decisions at the net, you have to use all the means open to you, to be in a ready position with the racket as the ball comes over the net. Apart from watching the ball from your opponent's racket, watch the angle of his racket: if it is coming under the ball he will play a lofted volley or a smash.

4. Not back to the ready position: Many intermediate players hit a volley and then either do not return to the center of the court, or in the case of a quick exchange, they do not get their racket back in the ready position for the next shot. Every volley must start with your guard up. The secrets of good volleying are sharp reflexes and dancing feet.

VOLLEY CHECKLIST

1. Wait in a crouching position with your eyes on the level of the ball.
2. Anticipate the direction of the ball by watching your opponent's racket level.
3. Use a short backswing and punch the ball.
4. Hit the ball in front of your forward foot and as close to the net as possible.

FOREHAND VOLLEY

To prepare for a forehand volley your left shoulder should turn towards the flight of the ball as soon as you have determined the ball is coming to the right. Pivot your hips ready to step forward as the ball comes over the net.

1 *Waiting position — shoulders leaning over toes.*

2 *Preparation — pivot and turn shoulder with short backswing.*

Step forward with your left foot as you want to take the ball as far in front of you as possible and this will help you keep your eyes on the ball. Hit the ball by punching forward, keeping the racket head above your wrist which should be firm on contacting the ball. Follow through out in front until your arm is fully stretched with the racket head facing the spot you wish the ball to go. Return immediately to the ready position

Of the current champions some of the most correct forehand volleyers are Brian Gottfield, John Newcombe, Vitas Gerulaitis, Martina Navratilova and promising junior Anne Smith. All these players have quick reflexes, move well to the ball, hit the volley well out in front, and bend their knees for the low ball. Of course they are all net rushers and therefore get more practice on their volley than the baseliners do.

BACKHAND VOLLEY

To prepare for the backhand volley, the right shoulder should turn immediately the ball leaves the opponent's racket and you have decided to take it on the backhand side. Your head must be still facing up the court towards the ball. As you turn completely and just before the hit your shoulder comes back

under your chin and at full stretch. You should be in the ready-to-step-forward position before the ball comes over the net, then step forward and throw your shoulder at and through the ball until your arm is fully extended. Your racket must finish pointing down the court towards the spot you wish the ball to go. You should feel as you come into your backhand volley that you are about to give someone a backhander or karate hit.

Your check point is the finish of the racket. If it is pointing towards the side fence, then your preparation was too late and you had to hit with your arm and not your shoulder. Immediately you have finished the shot, come back to the waiting position. If you are in a stationary position with your racket ready to come into the ball before it comes over the net, you can choose your own shot. That is, hit down the line, cross court or drop volley.

The aim is to get as close to the net as possible, hitting the ball at its full height, thus opening more angles for your return. The moment the ball starts dropping you are at a disadvantage and have to make a defensive volley by hitting it up and over the net. This means the ball loses the speed off the court and gives your opponent more time to get to it. This disadvantages you for the next shot by

3 *Step towards the net with shoulder under chin.*

4 *Hit the ball out in front, eyes on the ball.*

giving your opponent this extra time, and he can lob or pass you more easily.

Although they do not play as much tennis these days, the two classic backhand volleyers in the last decade have been Ken Rosewall and Tony Roche. Of the female players Evonne Goolagong (Cawley), and Billie Jean King have superb backhand volleys.

All of these players play their backhand volley well around sideways to the net and their shoulder turn brings their back almost facing the opponent. This solid shoulder hit or throw gives them the power in the shot and also the disguise, as with the same action they can play the shot down the line, cross court or use a drop volley.

BACKHAND VOLLEY CHECKLIST

1. Wait with your body low.
2. Pull the right shoulder under your chin as your arm comes back to full stretch.
3. Step forward and throw your arm at and through the ball.
4. Follow through with your racket pointing in the direction you wish the ball to go.

5 *Follow through with shoulder.*

SPIN AND SLICE

Bjorn Borg about to bring the racket up behind the ball in a brushing movement to achieve top spin. Photo courtesy Peter Meyers.

It is important for the beginner to learn how to hit flat shots first. A flat shot is a generalization of a classic stroke as there is very little chance of any shot being hit absolutely flat. When your swing is well groomed, then you can experiment with slice and top spin. Many champions play with almost no spin on their ground strokes at all. Good examples of this are Jimmy Connors and Chris Evert.

The serve is the one stroke in which most top players use spin of some kind. They usually use slice or top spin on the second serve as this cuts down the margin for error more than a fast, flat serve. While the high kick, twist serve is very hard to handle for the receiver, it is also a difficult shot to master and is used much more by men than women, who tend to use the slice serve for their second delivery. It is vital to get your first serve in when playing doubles, therefore it is good tactics to use a spin or slice service for the first delivery. This will give you more time when following your serve in, to take up a close position to the net for your first volley.

Many players develop a slight natural top spin, arriving out of the classic flat drive by coming over the ball slightly at contact and by bringing the racket over the ball in the follow through. This action helps keep the ball in the court, if you are playing with the wind behind you, or when playing in a high altitude. The heavy top spin as used by Bjorn Borg and Guillermo Vilas, needs a great deal of practice and a strong wrist. The method of achieving this action on both forehand and backhand, is to bring the racket up behind the ball in a brushing movement, finishing with the wrist rolling the racket over the top of the ball.

The reverse of top spin is underspin or slice. This is achieved by coming under the ball at the moment of impact, with the racket face slightly open. It cuts down the power of the stroke but gives more control. A slice on either forehand or backhand provides a good approach shot, when hit deep and down the line in singles, or a good return to the feet of the net rushing opponent in singles and doubles. In both instances the ball must be hit on the rise or the top of the bounce to make the ball skid through low on landing. Be sure to take a full follow through as with your ground strokes.

Martina Navratilova coming under the ball with racket face slightly open for an underspin backhand. Photo courtesy Russ Adams.

TWO-HANDED SHOTS

The two-handed backhand is generally not taught, but it has become popular today with so many children starting to play at an early age. It is very difficult to buy a light racket with a small enough grip, and often the player's wrist is not strong enough to hit the ball with one hand, particularly on the backhand side.

There are advantages in hitting a two-handed shot but also disadvantages. The vital factor in a good two-handed shot is the grip. Many people think they can pick up a racket with any grip and use two hands. Nothing could be more wrong. If you wish to use a two-handed backhand you must first put your right hand on top of the grip in either an Eastern backhand or a Continental grip, then put your left hand on the grip above this as though you were about to hit a left-handed forehand. Some players overlap the grip, holding the forefinger of the right hand with the little finger of the left hand. If you want to hit a two-handed forehand, just reverse the sequence; left hand on top of the grip as in a left handed backhand and the right hand above as an Eastern forehand grip.

There are several reasons to hit a backhand with two hands. The support of the second hand overcomes the problem of a weak wrist, and it gives precision and disguise to the shot. The two wrists reinforce each other to hold firm even when hitting a hard or deep shot, and the solidarity gives the precision. The greatest advantage is the two-handed shot naturally pulls the front shoulder inward and under the chin on the backswing. This prevents the elbow leading the swing and keeps the head still on the hit. These are the most common errors in a single handed shot. Good two-handed players use their shoulders and legs to full advantage, and by keeping their shoulders behind the shot it also gives them more power.

The first disadvantage of the double handed shot is the lack of stretch (reach) on this side, which means an extra step has to be taken on every shot to reach the ball, therefore you will have to be extra fast. The second disadvantage is the volley. Apart from the shortened stretch that a two-handed shot permits, two-handed players are particularly vulnerable in a quick volley exchange, because of the need to change grips. The tactics generally used by opponents to a two-handed volleyer is to hit the ball straight at them.

The greatest exponents of the two-handed shots on all surfaces are Chris Evert, Jimmy Connors and Bjorn Borg, all extremely quick movers.

Jimmy Connors demonstrates complete concentration on his two-handed backhand. Photo courtesy Peter Meyers.

THE ADVANCED STROKES

To be a complete player you must have a wide variety of strokes and the following need to be added to your repertoire, once you have mastered the basic strokes. These are the half volley, dropshot, drop volley and the lob volley. Once you have these you may wish to experiment with spin.

THE HALF VOLLEY

If you play a net game you will certainly need this stroke in your repertoire. However it should only be played as an emergency shot, to get you out of an awkward situation such as being caught halfway to the net, usually called "no man's land". Most average players find this a very difficult shot to play but it need not be if constructed correctly. The half volley is actually a ground stroke with the same fundamentals as the forehand and backhand but played with a very short backswing. As you are coming to the net on the move, the ball is very low so the shorter the swing the better, as

THE HALF VOLLEY

1 Sideways to the net, knees bent, short backswing.

THE DROP SHOT

1 Turn shoulder and pivot hips.

2 Step forward — short backswing.

2 *Hit the ball on the rise and out in front, with knees bent low.*

3 *Long follow through.*

3 *Racket face open, ready to come under ball.*

4 *Push forward in follow through.*

THE LOB VOLLEY

1 *Turn shoulders and pivot.*

2 *Short backswing.*
THE DROP VOLLEY

5 *Follow through, going up under ball.*

1 *Turn shoulder and pivot with short back-swing.*

3 *Sideways stance, eyes on ball and racket face at angle.*

4 *Start of follow through.*

2 *Racket face slightly open to take the pace off the ball.*

3 *Knees bent, eyes on the ball throughout the hit.*

the ball has to be hit on the rise and early preparation is vital. It is essential to play this shot with the knees bent very low on the hit and make sure you stay down in this position until the finish of the follow through. If your opponent is on the baseline then it is important to make a full follow through otherwise you will lose your depth and be passed on the next shot. The same action should be played even if your opponent has followed this shot to the net. In this case you need not hit it as hard but do not cut off your follow through, aim the ball at his feet low over the net. Keep moving in close to the net as your half volley has put you in a defensive position and hopefully you will force your opponent to hit up to you and so take up the offensive.

There are many more half volleys played in doubles than singles for the following reason. If the four of you are at the net and you play a lofted volley your opponent will hit this at your feet and you will need a good lightning-quick half volley to hit it back.

In singles played from the baseline you may receive an occasional ball just inside the baseline, which catches you unawares. This will force you to hit a half volley return so it is certainly a good shot to learn. A good way to practice the half volley is to stand side on and drop the ball just in front of your left foot, timing your forward swing to hit the ball on the rise and not forgetting to bend your knees and follow through.

THE DROP SHOT

The drop shot is a touch shot that should be hit only when the ball has bounced about midway between the baseline and the service court or between the service court and the net. The idea being to bring your baseline opponent to the net in order to pass or lob, or to play short to the open court when your opponent has been forced into the opposite corner at the baseline. The fundamentals are the same as for the forehand and backhand until the actual contact with the ball. Just as you come to the contact point, open the face of the racket a little and come under the ball, taking the pace off it and gently pushing it towards the place you wish it to fall. This slice under the ball will give the quick drop after the ball hits the ground. There should be a short follow through, more like catching the ball on the strings and pushing it over the net. The same applies as in other shots but it is much easier to execute this stroke if you take it on top of the bounce, preferably at net height; otherwise you have to lift it up and over the net, giving your opponent more time to recover. The timing and feel of a drop shot is so delicate it needs to be hit while stationary with the eyes fixed on the ball.

THE DROP VOLLEY

The drop volley is a more difficult stroke than the drop shot because of the extra touch required. It is a drop shot taken in the air and hit so that it just drops over the net, forcing your opponent to hit the ball up, and giving you a put away volley. If you hit it too high you will almost certainly lose the point. To hit a drop volley prepare as though you were about to hit a normal forehand or backhand volley. Just as you stroke the ball bring your racket head underneath it and take the pace off the ball. Hold the ball on the racket and just push it gently over the net. The face of the racket coming under the ball should provide the back spin necessary to make the ball drop sharply on your opponent's side of the net. There is practically no follow through on this shot.

THE LOB VOLLEY

The lob volley is the most difficult stroke in the game and is not used often. It is a shot that should be played as a surprise shot in a volleying exchange, in either singles or doubles, to force your opponent back from the net. Like the drop volley the lob volley calls for great touch. The chances of error are fairly high and if you miss you had better duck. To hit a lob volley you prepare the same as for a forehand or backhand volley. As you bring the racket forward open your racket face to hit under the ball and then push it up and over your opponent's head. Keep your wrist and arm firm and follow through, up and under the ball. You will have to judge how hard to hit it. If you take this shot off a slow ball you will need to hit it harder than off a fast ball.

STRATEGY

With her eyes fixed on the ball, Evonne
Goolagong Cawley ensures perfect timing for
this backhand. Photo courtesy Peter Meyers.

STRATEGY

WATCHING THE BALL

Many players do not realize that the eyes commence the chain reaction of eye to mind to muscle. If you do not use the first the others will not happen. Your eyes should be used as your camera. To take a clear picture you must have them on the level of the ball, if you look down on the ball your picture will be out of focus. This is one of the advantages of concentrating on hitting the ball on the top of the bounce. Apart from helping your concentration, it is the split second the ball is stationary and a clear picture can be taken by the eye on a still object. A good exercise for this is to bounce the ball and catch it on your first and middle fingers. To do this you must catch it on the top of the bounce with a very still head. It may seem difficult at first but with practice you can do it and when you have mastered this you can catch it on one finger.

CONCENTRATION

Some people are able to concentrate more naturally than others, particularly those with a placid nature. However, it can be worked on just as any other condition and improved tremendously. One good technique is to put everything else out of your mind except the ball, after all you are playing the ball not your opponent, and that should be your prime target from the moment you walk on the court, even in the warm up. Shut out any home or business problems you might have on the way to the game. Do not let your opponent or his personality or anyone watching distract you. Clear your mind before each point. This is why some players bounce the ball before they serve. Start clearing your mind as you walk over to return the serve and do not get ready to receive until you have. Concentrate on each point as you play it, forget the error you might have just made, or the wrong line call by the umpire.

There must be nothing on your mind except the game in hand during the match. Remember, a good temperament produces a good competitor.

GAME STRATEGY

Tennis is a game of many facets and this is why it is so stimulating and interesting.

The game should be played like chess, the aim being to outwit and outmaneuver your opponent. There is no such thing as a mean shot, only a clever shot. The object of the game is to place the ball where it causes your opponent the greatest problems and allows you to exploit your strengths. Your opponent will in turn apply counter pressures. You should aim to dictate the game at all times, keeping your opponent on the move constantly to tire him out and keeping yourself fresh. Stamina may well be the vital difference between winning and losing.

Once in a match you should not try to practice strokes. All your practice should have been done before that, on the practice court. During a match your mind should be free to concentrate on the ball, and on strategy.

If possible, try to see your opponent play before the match so you are aware of his strengths and weaknesses. If you can't do this, then use the warm-up time before the match for this purpose. Send him down a variety of shots: low and high bouncing balls to forehand and backhand; a mid court ball and a drop shot; forehand and backhand volleys. Note his weaknesses and keep this information stored in your mind so you can play him an appropriate shot at a vital point — say a 30-all point, or if you are down a game point.

If you haven't made these assessments before the match starts you risk losing valuable games while you are working out his deficiencies.

Use the elements to your advantage. Make sure you have checked which way the wind is blowing before you go on the court. You will need to lob harder against the wind than with it. Do not make your shots so fine on a windy day. Aim a little further inside the line to allow for it. If it is blowing very hard, a down the middle of the court strategy in singles is a wise tactic.

If you play against a net rusher, you will be able to lob more when he is facing the sun as it is difficult to hit an overhead shot with the sun in your eyes.

SINGLES STRATEGY

Singles, the player to player contest, is a harder game both physically and mentally than doubles because one player has to cover all the court. There is no rest between points and no partner with whom to discuss tactics. To play tournament singles you must be in good condition, which means practicing at least three sets in a row for ladies and five for men, as well as an off court conditioning program to build up stamina and muscles.

Most players play their best singles when they are young and have peak power and agility. However, this does not mean that older or club players cannot enjoy a singles game, particularly if they play against players of their own standard. Quite often an older player will beat a younger player with clever strategy. Familiarize yourself with the court and the trajectory of the ball in relation to it. It is a well known fact that more than 50% of points are lost on errors, so do not try to play a shot that geometrically will never go over the net or in the court. It is necessary to assess your own game, taking note of your strengths and weaknesses.

Do not rush the net on your serve if it is not strong enough to put your opponent at a disadvantage, or if your backhand and forehand volleys and overhead smash are not solid shots.

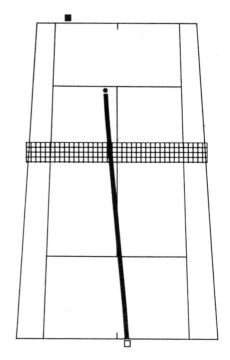

1 *Serve down the center.*

SINGLES ATTACKING TACTICS FROM THE NET

To play an attacking net game by following your serve to the net is much easier on a fast surface such as grass or synthetics than on a clay court. If you are serving to the forehand court the percentage serve is down the center. This has two advantages, first it gives a smaller range of angle for the return, and second you will be aiming for the backhand which is generally the weaker stroke. Follow your serve to the net in line with the ball and pause slightly when you have reached the center of the court to assess the direction of the return. Then move to the side the ball is coming to, prepared to make first volley taking it as early as you can as it comes over the net. If you have to hit the first volley up, make sure you get the ball deep to the baseline and move back to the center of the court as quickly as you can. If the receiver has stayed back he will have to hit the ball up to

you and you should be able to place the volley away. When serving to the backhand court, aim most of your deliveries to the far backhand corner. Most net rushers prefer to stand close to the center line when serving to the backhand court as it gives them a straight line to run to the net. You can get a better angle by standing 6 feet (2 meters) from the center but it also gives your opponent a better angle for return and leaves more room for the up the line shot. It also advertises to the opponent the server's intention of serving a wide ball.

DEFENDING AGAINST THE VOLLEYER

If your opponent has a strong service you are in a defensive situation and should try to get the ball back low over the net, using your "dink" shot preferably on an angle. You then will have to wait for the next shot to play a

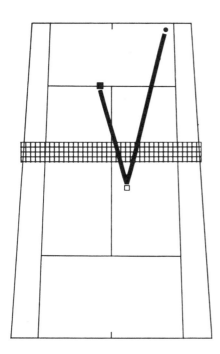

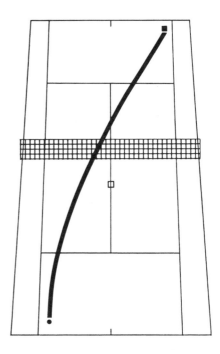

2 *Receiver returns low.*
Server volleys deep.

3 *Receiver lobs deep to backhand corner.*

passing shot or lob. A good lob over the backhand side deep in the corner will then put you on the attack. When your opponent misses his first serve, move in 1 or 2 paces from the baseline: this will give you the opportunity to step around the serve and go for a low wide passing shot. Do not panic or let yourself be rushed when hitting the shot. This tactic also pressures him into trying for more depth and you may force him into a double fault. You will need even more attention on the ball, such as watching it longer throughout the hit, because your shot needs to be more accurate.

ATTACKING AND DEFENDING FROM THE BASELINE OR STAYING BACK AFTER SERVING

To the forehand court the percentage serve is down the center. Apart from being on the opponent's backhand, which is often the weakness, it cuts down his option of shots because of the lessening of angles; from this position it is very difficult to hit a winner off even an average second serve. It is advisable to serve occasionally wide to the forehand side even if he or she has a strong forehand, if only to keep your opponent guessing and not allow him to get set for a certain shot. Of course, if your opponent has a weak forehand you can place more serves in that direction.

When serving to the backhand court aim most of your deliveries to the backhand corner and keep your variation for the one down the center. Depending on where the return comes back, you may have to engage in a number of rallies before you force your opponent into an error or hit a winner. Hit the ball with as much depth as you can and into the corners. These are the most difficult shots to return and will keep your opponent on the move.

SINGLES NET ATTACK TO DEUCE COURT

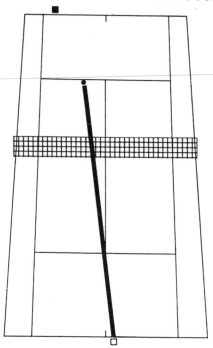

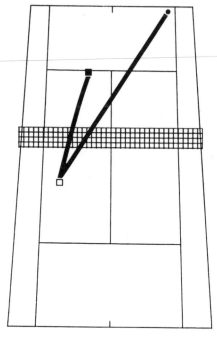

1 *Serve down the center.
Receiver returns up the line.*

2 *Server volleys deep cross court*

SINGLE NET ATTACK TO ADVANTAGE COURT

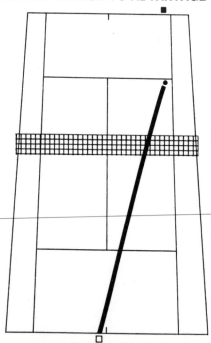

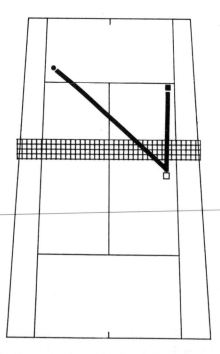

1 *Serve deep to backhand.
Receiver returns up the line.*

2 *Server returns deep, forcing weak return.*

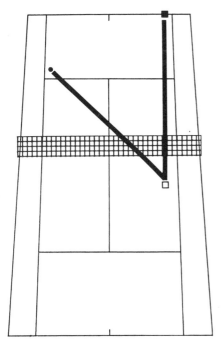

3 *Receiver returns up line.*
Server volleys angle winner.

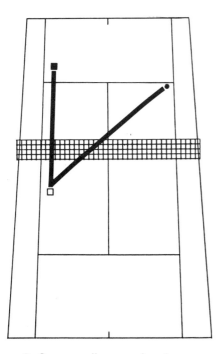

3 *Server volleys angle winner.*

If the ball is short you may be forced to go to the net. Most of the baseline games are played on clay or slow synthetic surfaces. The golden rule is, do not go for a winner unless the ball lands between the service line and the net. To try for a clean winner from the baseline is very risky. This policy is shown clearly in long matches on clay with such players as Vilas, Borg and Connors. These players only venture to the net when they are forced to on the short ball.

An effective attacking shot from the base line is "wrong footing". This means to play a series of shots either deep to the corners or at wide sharp angles and as your opponent runs back to the center of the court expecting the ball on the other side, hit the ball to the spot he has just left and catch him going the wrong way. Even if he does get back to the ball you will get an easy shot to make a winner.

Tennis players use a baseline game for two reasons: either they have a weak volley, or they are not fast enough to get to the net quickly. Therefore, a good strategy is to use a drop shot to bring your opponent to the net and play a passing shot, lob, or even hit it straight at them if their reflexes are slow.

Keep the ball in play: Lew Hoad always said, "Get the ball over no matter how: just make sure you win the last point." Cut down your own errors and you will give yourself a better chance of winning the match. There is nothing more irritating than an opponent who never makes an unforced error. Chris Evert and Jimmy Connors are great examples of this.

Play to the open court: Whether you are advancing to the net or playing from the baseline, a ball deep in the corners is the most difficult to return. Your objective is to dictate the game by making your opponent run as much as you can, endeavoring to tire him out. If you are playing a baseliner, a drop shot is a very handy weapon and can win many points particularly if your opponent has been forced wide into a corner. However, do not use it against a net rusher as you are giving him the opportunity he has been waiting for to attain the net position.

Hit the ball early: Make sure you hit the ball at the earliest possible time. If it's a volley move into position as the ball is coming over the net and hit it at its full height. Once you have let it drop low you will have to hit a defensive shot. At all times you should be hitting down to your opponent and making him hit up to you. Most

ATTACKING THE SERVER WHO STAYS BACK IN SINGLES

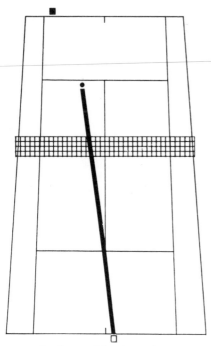

1 *Server hits down line.*

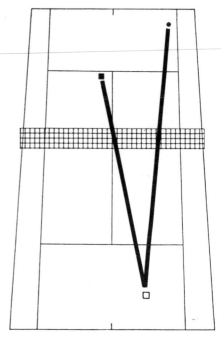

2 *Return ball deep into backhand corner.*

club players take the return of serve far too late. Try to hit it on top of the bounce, remembering that the serve has to land within the service line half way up the court. This will enable you to use the pace from your opponent's shot so you will not have to hit it so hard and it will give you better timing and maximum speed for less energy. Hitting earlier and further forward will always give your opponent less time to recover.

Attack the weakness: Everyone has a weakness in his or her game or at least one stroke less deadly than another. You will have assessed this in the warm up by testing your opponent's strokes even if you are not familiar with his or her game. Play to this stroke whenever you are down a point.

Change a losing game: If you are losing, change your tactics completely. If your opponent is net rushing, lob more. If you are being outplayed from the baseline, try advancing to the net. If your opponent is enjoying your fast drives, take the pace off the ball by playing a few slow shots to disturb his rhythm.

A golden rule: Never change a winning game, but always change a losing game.

SERVING AND STAYING BACK IN SINGLES

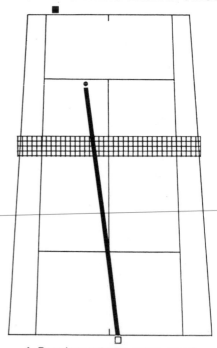

1 *Receiver returns cross court. Server hits down line.*

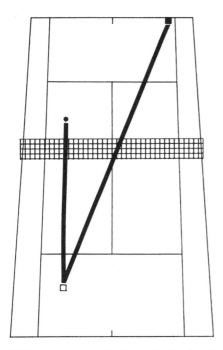

3 *Move in to net behind flight of ball.*

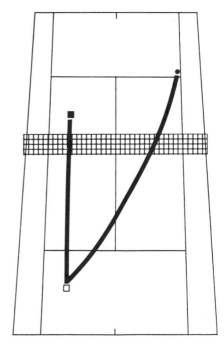

4 *Angle volley cross court.*

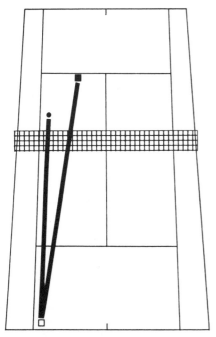

2 *Receiver plays cross court.*
Server plays short ball.

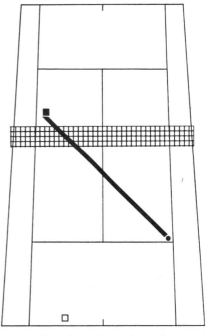

3 *Receiver plays down line.*
Server can lob or pass.

DOUBLES STRATEGY

ATTACKING THE SERVER WHO STAYS BACK IN DOUBLES

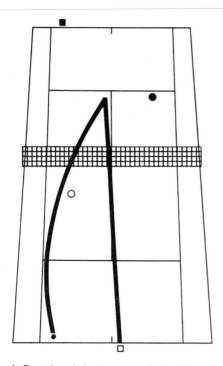

1 *Receiver lobs to server's backhand.*

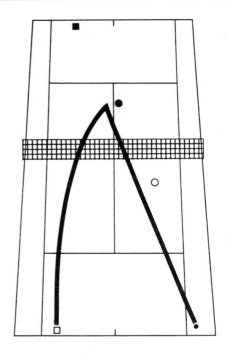

2 *Server lobs.*
Receiver's partner angle smashes.

Doubles play is important particularly to the young and the club player. Apart from top tournament players, the average tennis enthusiast plays doubles 90% of the time. In fact weekend and ladies' mid-week competitions are all doubles games. Doubles does not need quite the same stamina and fleetness of foot as singles, but it does require precision and a quick brain. There are now two players to cover the court at the other end and good placements are a must.

Doubles calls for teamwork; the two partners should preferably be of the same standard and have a thorough knowledge of each other's game and be confident in each other's ability. Knowing your partner is important. Some people like to discuss tactics during a match and others lose their concentration if they chat too much. However, you should always be prepared to say "mine" or "yours" and call "back" if you send up a lob from the baseline and he or she is at the net. You should tell each

other your plans: if your partner is serving and you intend to intercept (poach), then warn him before he serves or you will both end up going for the same ball. You must be unselfish to play doubles, in fact your duty is to make the set up for your partner, not yourself. Many players feel cheated when they play a number of good shots and their partner gets the acclaim for putting away the sitter, but this is as it should be. He, of course, should be trying to do the same for you.

When choosing sides, the player with the better forehand should play in the forehand court and the player with the stronger backhand should play the backhand court. Generally it is advisable for the stronger player to play the backhand court as he will have the mid court smash and volley to put away. He is also playing the pressure game point. Doubles is a game that is won at the net. Two good net players will always beat two good baseliners, even on a slow surface. The whole basis of the

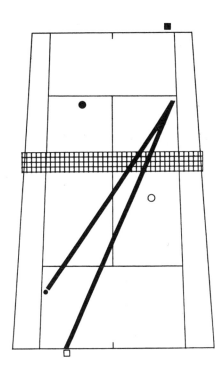

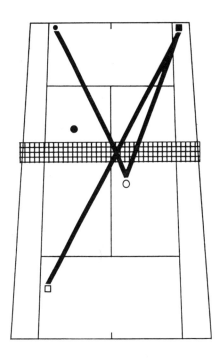

1 *Serve deep to backhand.*
Receiver returns cross court.

2 *Server returns deep, forcing weak return.*
Partner volleys winner.

game is to hit the ball down to your opponents and make them hit the ball up to you for the put away shot. Therefore the server should always follow his serve to the net, on both first and second serves. There would be many more champions if players began following their serve to the net when they first started to play. Once you become proficient at covering half the court and coming to the net on your serve, you will be amazed how this will help your singles game at the net. The server should only have to cover his or her half of the court. His aim is to get to the net as quickly as possible, to volley the ball before it starts to drop, to enable him to hit it down to his opponent. This means a player must cover his own lob. It is a golden rule in doubles that each player is responsible for taking the lob over his head, running back to the baseline for it if necessary; otherwise it puts your team out of position.

Many club players disadvantage themselves at the start by standing in the wrong positions

on the court. When serving in doubles it is best to stand half way between the center mark and the singles sideline. That way you are dividing the coverage of the court, by you and your partner, and dividing your opponent's options in half. From this position you have the shortest distance to run to the net, or if you stay back you can reach the lob over your partner's head, or a wide angle return. Your partner should stand about 6 feet (2 meters) from the net and a few paces in from the singles sideline. When you are receiving serve you should stand on the baseline and just inside the singles sideline on the forehand court. Of course if your opponent's best serve is a wide slice then you should stand over a little, but you will be leaving the center open. On the backhand court you should stand about 3 feet (1 meter) in from the sideline. Many errors are made off the backhand return by the receiver standing too far to the left and then having to jam his backhand swing. When the server misses with his first serve, the receiver should immediately move in two or three paces as the server will seldom take the risk of a fast second serve. Remember that the ball has to bounce inside the service line and you should be taking it on the rise or the top of the bounce.

In a doubles match the receiver's partner should stand just inside the service line and a few paces in from the sideline. As soon as the receiver hits the ball, his partner should move in towards the net along with the flight of the ball. If the receiver makes a weak return to the net player, this enables his partner to cover that side of the court, and not leave a gap. If the receiver hits a good, low return, his partner should move in as close to the net as possible, to be in a position to hit his opponent's return for a winner.

A fast serve is not as effective in doubles as in singles play; a well placed, medium paced deep serve is the most effective. Concentrate on getting your first serve in. If you miss with this your opponent will step in on your second serve, giving him the advantage to hit the ball down and so making you volley up and play a defensive shot. The best percentage shot when you are serving into the forehand court is down the center to the receiver's backhand unless your opponent is left handed, because you give him less angle on the return and it is a difficult shot for him to hit up the sideline.

This can also give your partner a chance for an intercept on his forehand volley where he has a longer reach. To the backhand court it is usually better to serve wide to your opponent's backhand, but certainly serve one down the center occasionally to keep him guessing.

The return of serve is as important as the serve itself. Nobody can win a match without breaking their opponent's service. The hardest ball for the server when he is coming in is the low, slow ball at his feet and this shot is difficult for his partner at the net to intercept. As an alternative use your lob, particularly if the serve is difficult to return. Better to send up a high lob, giving yourself a chance to get back into position, than give your opponent a set up. Do not forget to use your lob as an offensive shot as well. If the opposing net player is worrying you by intercepting, play a shot down his sideline. This is a risky shot as the net is 6 inches (15 cm) higher here than in the middle, but it is worth it to keep him guessing.

The doubles strategy is completely different for players who feel their serve and volley are inadequate to allow them to come to the net. You must be prepared for much longer rallies. The lob from the forehand court is the most

ATTACKING THE NET RUSHER

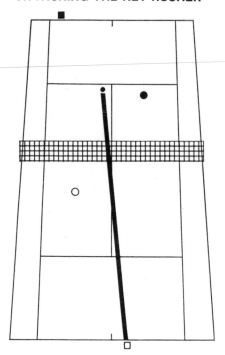

1 *Serve to backhand. Dink (drop shot).*

DOUBLES ATTACKING THE NET

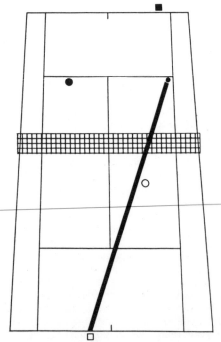

1 *Serve down center, move quickly to net.*

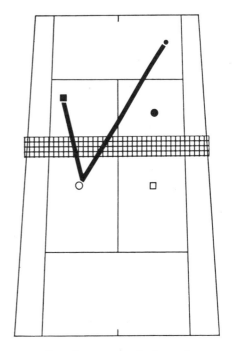

2 *Server forced to lift return*

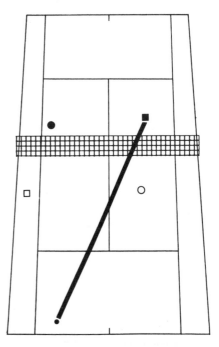

3 *Receiver moves in for volley.*

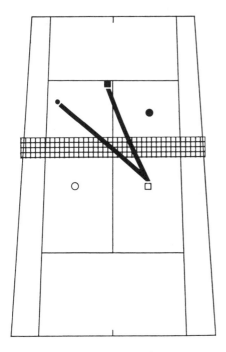

2 *Volley down to receiver's feet.*

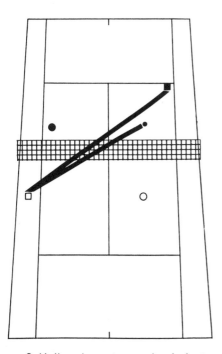

3 *Server's partner volleys return down center.*

attacking shot. It means the server has to turn around and move to the other side of the court, forcing his partner to change sides. After playing this shot you have two choices: you can move into the net for the smash or high volley return, or you now have the advantage of playing your forehand up the line to your opponent's backhand, and your partner will have the loose volley coming on his forehand volley side, whilst your opponent's partner has less reach for his backhand volley.

If you return cross court make your return deep, to give your partner a chance for an easy volley. Do not play more than one shot back to the player, make them move to the ball. A drop shot or short angle will be more awkward for them to return and in this case your partner must watch his sideline.

The return from the backhand court is a little more restricted as the lob is not quite as effective, having to pass the net player's right handed smashing side, and it is thus on the server's forehand. The basic return from this side is the deep cross court, varying with an angle or drop shot. The drop shot, or "dink" return from the backhand court is more effective than from the forehand court as it is more concealed and on the opponent's backhand.

When serving to the forehand court and staying on the baseline, the percentage serve is down the center, however, you can serve more wide serves as you are now forcing a sharp angled return or lob and they will not present such difficulties when you are at the back of the court. Serving to the backhand court you can serve more down the center, as the opponent's forehand return down the middle will be easier to handle from the baseline.

MIXED DOUBLES

Although mixed doubles has been overshadowed at the professional level by the big money tennis in recent years, it is still a very entertaining spectator game when the stars play, and an enjoyable game socially or at Association Competition standard. Unfortunately in Australia the National and State Championships have deleted this event, although Wimbledon and the U.S. Nationals have retained it.

In social mixed doubles the man may decide to serve a slower delivery to the woman and not slam an easy shot at her. However once you play competition the attitude must change, and the weaker play must be exploited; in most cases this means playing the woman.

The principles of mixed doubles play are the same as for men's or women's doubles. If the players are of the same grade the man should take the backhand court and the woman the forehand court, even if the woman is left handed. A man usually has a longer reach and is stronger on the overhead smash. As in any other doubles play the woman should smash or chase back any lob over her own head. Even if she does not put the ball away for a winner it will leave her team in a better position for the next shot. The man should be following his serve to the net. If he is forced to run back for his partner's lob he cannot concentrate on getting in close to the net for his first vital volley and eventually will probably end up halfway in, wondering about the lob.

This strategy is just what your opponents have been planning. The man will now have to play half volleys, an easy target for the opposing man for a put away shot. Any easy shot down the center should be left to the man if both partners are in a position to play it. It is folly for the woman to try to outplay the male opposition in a volley exchange and most smashes should be directed towards the woman's side of the court. Of course, if the man is weaker than the woman the reverse applies. The basic principle of doubles is for the forehand court player to "dink" (drop shot) return the serve or lob and this is even more important in mixed tennis as it gives the man on the backhand court more opportunities to intercept or poach at the net. A team that follow all their serves to the net, providing they can volley adequately, will always beat the back court team. Many women feel their serve and volley are inadequate to come to the net on, especially serving to the male opposition. If this is so it is advisable to concentrate on getting the first serve in, otherwise the man will step in on the second serve and make a good deep shot to the backhand corner. By the time you hit it he will be camped on the net and it is a very difficult shot to return low. If you are forced into a defensive shot in mixed doubles it is always better to play a high, deep lob, than a high drive for the man to kill.

Most men find it easy to intercept or poach the return from the woman's side. If you find this happening the lob is the best answer, aimed anywhere high, at the baseline will do. By doing this you may force a weak return for your partner to smash. Another way to "keep him honest" is an early side line shot and this will make him tentative about running across. In average competition play, the general rule is for the woman to work at a strategy to make an easy shot for the man to put away.

EQUIPMENT,
TRAINING AND
PRACTICE

SELECTING EQUIPMENT

There are many different types of tennis racket and it is vital that you select one that has the correct grip size and weight and is strung to the tension that suits your game.

SELECTING A TENNIS RACKET

For a tennis player the most important purchasing decision you will make is the selection of your racket. Many people like to give rackets as a gift but this is unwise. A racket should be personally selected and tried as one would a dress or suit. Before you buy a new racket try out as many models as you can. Borrow rackets if you can, to find one racket that suits your size and style of play. Many people ask about the differences and advantages between wood, metal and fibreglass rackets. A good wooden racket is packed in the throat with leather and wood, softer materials than metal, so there is less jar on the arm and more control of the ball. However the ball will leave the metal racket faster. The choice is up to you. It is important to choose the correct grip size and weight and have the racket strung to the tension that suits your game.

Hold the handle in the "shake hands" grip — your thumb should sit comfortably on the first knuckle of your middle or index finger. Too small or too large a grip may give you a tennis elbow; in either case you have to grip too tight. The weight should be even or slightly to the handle: you can judge this by balancing the racket on your finger in the centre of the frame. The maximum weight strung would be 13½ oz (383 g) and lighter if you are small. Most male champions use no heavier than this, as timing and rhythm give the power to the stroke, not a heavy racket.

After choosing the frame, have it strung to your desired tension. Champions and most grade players prefer gut as it is more resilient; however, there are good synthetics on the market. Whilst tension is a personal choice, a racket strung between 55 and 60 pounds (25-27 kg) will give you plenty of zip and still enable you to have control. If the strings are too tight the resilience is pulled out of the gut.

As rackets are expensive, they need to be looked after. Use a cover only to protect from rain: gut takes in moisture and the strings will sweat if left in a cover. Do not play in the rain unless you are prepared to replace the strings. Synthetics are not so affected by moisture and therefore are advisable for young people and are a must for night play outdoors. There is no good substitute for a leather grip but if you perspire freely it will need to be renewed once the top is worn off. The grip is just as important as any part of the racket.

Top quality tennis balls are sold in airtight cans so that they do not lose their pressure. Low standard balls will affect your game badly.

TENNIS BALLS

Reliable tennis ball manufacturers merchandise tennis balls in pressurized cans today. This method keeps the balls fresh indefinitely. Balls not in cans are apt to lose their pressure and you will not know how old the balls are. There is no substitute for a top quality tennis ball. Soft or low standard balls will not only affect your game badly, but also hurt your arm as you will have to hit much harder to gain power and zip off your racket. Hence the keeping of balls in an insulated box at the side of the court at Wimbledon and international matches. Purchase only balls that have your Association's seal of approval stamped on them and you will know they have been thoroughly tested to specifications. (See THE BALL, page 11).

TENNIS CLOTHES

When buying a shirt and shorts or dress swing your arms and bend as though you are playing to make sure you have freedom of movement across your shoulders and underarms. (If you are apt to change weight look for a style where

The ideal tennis shoe has a built-in arch support and a long front lacing. The soles should be approved for tennis courts.

seams may be adjusted.) The best sock is one with an absorbent foot; if ladies want to eliminate ankle marks they can wear pom-pom socks. When trying on tennis shoes, always take your socks with you as a comfortable fit is most important. Look for a shoe with a built in arch support and a long front lacing which will give you a better adjustment as your feet get hot. The soles should be approved for tennis courts. As synthetic courts are becoming more popular and are much harder on the feet, you may need more protection to prevent blisters; if so wear two pairs of socks or add another pair of insoles.

Make sure you have a cardigan, jumper or warm up jacket to put on at the conclusion of your game to prevent chills and tightening muscles. If you perspire freely, a sweatband will absorb the perspiration as it runs down your forearm, thus protecting your palm. A lot of tennis is played on extremely hot days and the length of time spent on the court is often underestimated, especially when playing a match. Therefore, it is wise to apply a non-greasy sun lotion to the exposed parts of the body. The back of the neck is the most vulnerable spot. If you feel the sun affecting you, wet a large handkerchief and tie it around your neck.

It is far better to wear a hat or a shade than sunglasses. Unless they have a perfect lens (and these are most expensive), they hamper your vision. Optical lenses, of course, are a different matter.

EXERCISE, TRAINING AND DIET

EXERCISES

1. To strengthen the calf muscles, stand at arm's length facing the wall, feet together, heels on the ground, palms on the wall. Push your pelvis forward and you will feel the pull on your calf muscles. Hold for 20 seconds and repeat.

2. To improve flexibility to hips and thighs, stand straight with legs wide apart. Slowly squat to the left, shifting all the weight to the left leg, keeping the right leg straight. Move slowly back to standing position. Repeat on right side. You should feel the stretch on your hips and thighs.

3. To help strengthen your back stretch action, lean against the wall with your right hand, take your right foot in your left hand and

lean your head back as far as possible. Hold for 20 seconds. Repeat with your left foot in your right hand.

4. For your back, lie face down with hands on shoulders. Raise the trunk and hands off the ground simultaneously.

5. Two good exercises for stomach muscles are:

A. Lie face down on the floor, place the palms of your hands on the floor, lift up, keeping legs and back straight, then lower yourself as close to the floor as you can without touching it. Start off with as many as possible and increase each day.

B. Lie on your back, hands behind your neck, then slowly bring your body forward, leaving your legs straight and

4

5B

5A

firmly on the floor. Stretch your finger tips out to touch your toes and try to put your chin on your knees. You will find you will get a little closer each day. Start with 10 and increase daily.

6. To strengthen your arms swing a dumbell or tennis racket.
7. For your wrists, squeeze an old tennis ball repeatedly.

TRAINING

If you wish to improve your tennis good physical condition and stamina will help you and you will also enjoy your games more without suffering from exhaustion or muscular ailments. It is not enough to just play tennis to keep in shape. Simple training may be done at home.

Running or running on the spot will improve your stamina. Skipping or jumping rope improve your footwork. Short sprints will help your breathing and quicken your take off.

DIET

The basic training diet adopted by most top players is grilled steaks and salads for main meals and omelettes, for lighter meals.

Always eat a good, nourishing meal the night before you play. The day of playing you should eat at least l½ hours before your game; your speed is reduced if the food is not digested. When playing a competition match, and you feel you need a snack, in between sets, eat a yoghurt or an apple, rather than sandwiches, hamburgers or cream cakes.

HOW TO PRACTICE

Hit forehands down line.

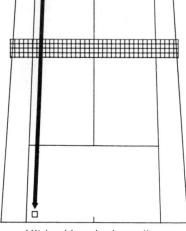

Hit backhands down line.

Hit lobs from baseline.

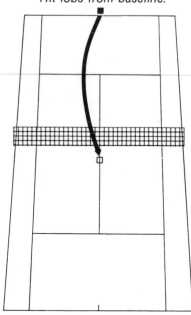

Hit smashes from the net.

For a person who has never played tennis, catching and throwing a ball will help to co-ordinate the eye/hand reflex. If you cannot catch a ball you will not be able to hit it. Swinging the racket is also good practice. You should pretend you are contacting the ball and the follow through should pull you face on towards the imaginary net. These actions will help develop your appropriate body muscles. When you are learning, try to practice with someone who will stand at the net and feed you the balls in a good position for hitting until your stroke becomes a reflex action. You could in turn do the same for them. When you are advanced enough to have practice sessions do not just hit the ball up and down the middle of the court. Commence with playing forehands across to each other. If your shots are not landing within a few paces of the baseline make sure you are not cutting off your follow through. Check that your racket head is finishing high and pointing to the spot on the court you are aiming for. When you are getting good depth returns to the center of the baseline after each shot, stand a little further to either side so you have to run to each ball. When you can do this consistently (say nine out of ten perfect shots) start hitting the ball down the line to your practice partner's backhand. Your practice partner then hits backhand down the line to your forehand.

Then change again and move to the other side of the court so you can hit backhand down the line to his forehand. Both players then move to the backhand court and play back-hands across court. If you do this continually with a dozen balls you will find it will build up your stamina and is more interesting than just running or jumping rope.

Move in then to half way between the service court and net and hit volleys to each other, trying to hit as many balls on the fly (full) as you can. Start slowly at first, gaining speed as you improve your reflexes. For advanced players, the one up at the net and two on the baseline routine is the best for sharpening up volleys and smashes. Conversely if you want to sharpen your baseline game have two in the volleying position and one on the baseline, playing every ball on the first bounce. Change positions alternately and do this as long as you can stand the pace. You can then practice your serve, letting your practice partner return the serve as his practice. After you have hit 20 serves to each side, change and let your partner serve to you. When you are satisfied with your serve follow it in and have your practice partner return to you, trying to volley it deeper each time. At first you may only get to the service line but as you get faster and more confident you should be able to get to a few paces from the net and so catch the ball on the way up. You should try to leave time after this therapy stlye practice to play one or two sets.

GLOSSARY OF INTERNATIONAL TERMS:

ACE: An unreachable ball when returning serve.

ADVANTAGE COURT: Left or backhand court.

ALLEY OR TRAMLINES: Alley is the American expression, Tramline is English or Australian. This is the area of the court between the doubles sideline and the singles sideline. The ball is out in singles but good in doubles.

APPROACH SHOT: A shot behind which the player advances to the net. It is not meant to end the point but to put the player in a good position to make the next shot a winning volley and his opponent in a bad position to hit a passing shot.

BACKHAND COURT: Left or advantage court.

BACKSWING: The arc or swing of the racket made preparatory to the forward swing to meet the ball.

BAND: The strip of canvas attached to the top of the net.

BASELINE: The backline at each end of the court.

CANNON BALL: A bullet-like serve.

CENTER MARK: The mark bisecting the baseline, defining one of the limits of the service position.

CENTER SERVICE LINE: The line dividing the service court in halves, and separating the right and left service courts.

CHIP SHOT: A ground stroke hit with a volley-like action with underspin.

CHOKE: A freezing up of normal strokes owing to nerves.

CLAY: A general term used for courts composed of clay, dirt, loose pebbles, or crushed shell.

CROSS COURT: A ball that is hit from one side of the court to the diagonally opposite side (in the case of two right handers, a forehand cross court would go to the opponent's forehand, and a backhand cross court to the opponent's backhand).

DEUCE: A score of 40 each.

DEUCE COURT: Right or forehand court.

DINK: A soft dipping shot that clears the net by a small margin and bounces low.

DOUBLES: A game of tennis played between four players.

DOUBLE FAULT: Failure of both first and second serve to go into the proper court, resulting in the loss of the point.

DOWN-THE-LINE: Hitting the ball in a line parallel to the sidelines. (If two right-handers are playing, a player hitting his forehand down the line would be hitting to his opponent's backhand. A player hitting his backhand down the line would be hitting to his opponent's forehand.)

DROP SHOT: A ball hit off a ground stroke with enough underspin to make it drop to the ground just after it clears the net, and to have very little or no forward motion after the bounce.

DRAW SHEET: A sheet that shows how players will meet in the tournament.

DROP VOLLEY: A shot similar to the drop shot except that it is hit off a volley.

FAULT: A served ball that does not strike in the proper court, or is not properly served.

FOLLOW THROUGH: The finish of a stroke after the racket has hit the ball.

FOOT FAULT: A fault on serve caused by one foot touching the line or stepping inside the court or going over the center mark before the ball is hit. Jumping in the air is not a foot-fault even if both feet are well in the court, provided neither foot makes contact with the ground before the ball is hit.

FOREHAND: A ball hit on the right side of the body by a right-hander or the left side of the body by a left-hander.

FOREHAND COURT: Right or deuce court.

FOUL SHOT: If a ball is struck twice, or is touched before it comes over the net, or a player touches the net, or a ball in play touches a player, or anything that he wears or carries falls into the opponent's court.

GAME POINT: A position in which a player needs only one point to win the game.

GRASS: A court composed of grass.

GRIP: The position of the hand in relation to the racket.

GROUND STROKE: A ball hit after it has bounced. Ground strokes can be either forehand or backhand.

GUT: Strings of the racket that are made from animals' intestines.

HACKER: A player of nondescript tennis ability.

HALF VOLLEY: A ball hit just after the bounce when it is as low as 6 inches (15 cm), off the ground. It is actually not a volley but a ground stroke.

IN PLAY: A ball is "in play" from the moment at which it is delivered in service until the point has been completed.

LOVE: A nil score

LEFT COURT: Backhand or advantage court.

LET: A call to re-play the point. When the ball hits the net on serve, but lands in the proper service court, a let is called and the first or second serve is replayed. A let is also called because of interruption of play, such as a ball rolling into the court from another court.

MATCH POINT: The time in a match when a player is one point away from winning.

MIXED DOUBLES: A game of tennis where opposing pairs each consist of a man and a woman.

NET: The netting placed across the middle of the court.

NO MAN'S LAND: The area of the court between the serving line and 3 feet (1 meter) inside the baseline.

NOT UP: When a player fails to reach a ball on the first bounce.

NYLON: Strings made of nylon in the racket instead of gut. Good for wet weather or night play.

ON THE LINE: The call that means the ball was good. A ball is still in play as long as it touches any part of the line.

ON THE RISE: Taking the ball as it is coming off the ground when it has not yet reached its full height.

OPEN STANCE: Feet facing the net as the ball is hit.

OVERHEAD OR SMASH: A ball hit when it is over the area of the head with a swing similar to the service.

PASSING SHOT: A ball that passes the net player. The three passing shots are the cross court, down the line and the lob.

PERCENTAGE TENNIS: Playing the shots or using the strategy that gives you the best chance to win.

PERMANENT FIXTURES: The umpire, linesmen, spectators and their chairs or stands, ball boys (when in their respective places) net, posts, back and side stops, and any other objects situated around the court.

PLACEMENT: An untouchable winner off a ground stroke, volley or overhead but not off a serve.

POINT: The smallest unit of the score.

POST: One of the wooden or metal uprights supporting the net.

POWER: The speed of the ball.